Selection of Poems

*

Traumear

*

Paperback ISBN 978-0-244-99072-5

*

www.traumear.com

*

The nameless beauty that clings to all I see.
What is death? A sieve. A filter.
And pain? Well, together we shall get through it.

(from page 8)

*

Pain into image

A callous tongue cannot speak
pretty poetry, nice poetry,
however it might get away with
the odd home truth.

Like a microlight on an updraft,
my guardian angel, called enthusiasm,
transports me to altitudes from where
I can see mankind clearly.

Some have a fairground mentality
that allows them to deal with hardship
playfully, however they lack character
and the truth avoids them.

Others need company
before they can enjoy themselves
but on their own they make sense
of much that does the world good.

I recognize the silly man
who is open to scandal and gossip
but sometimes by accident
he eases the strain for others.

Take the sage now who sits
quietly and bothers no one,
however then his disciples argue
over who understands him best.

The so-called lover of women
treads his promiscuous path
until one day a fine lady
comes to terms with her humanity.

I arrest every impulse in me
that would cause me to discount my pain
and yet as gravity claims me
I treat myself to a vicarious nap.

Ships on a turbulent ocean –
storms ordain their speed
and the vigilant lighthouse keeper
rocks back and forth in his chair.

Skyscrapers crash to earth,
the sun shines as heretofore,
warming the backs of gulls,
dispensing general contentment.

Fox cubs hurry across the roof,
our tarnished eyes espy them,
we reach for our gun, from its muzzle
a single compassion rose protrudes.

Salt on a slug’s back
is torture incomparable,
is the hypocrite’s fate at last
in the august presence of the master.

Oh this stale city air
and everyone living on the hog's back
for the moment, to be sure
and that eternal tra la la la laa!

Geese heading north
on the pillow of a south wind
and Christ's dearest rotting
in prisons and hospitals.

A hare squealing in a trap,
vomiting onto the grass
as the sun gleams on a droplet
of dew on a spider's web.

Contagious are the efforts of the rich
and the wine of the poor is sour
but the bricklayer knows his craft,
his behaviour is always conscientious.

Now the advancing cavalry
called age is a boon if we know
how rapidly we decline in security
under the spell of our prejudices.

A forest of emotion is uprooted
and discarded by neglectful behaviour
while care broadens our outlook
and touches our hearts specifically.

*

Two verses each for Erika and Jack

(to be recited)

I

Childish fun

Well might you ask, what is more fun,
climbing into our tree house where
the world is ours, secret and fair

or wading knee deep in the stream
digging out treasures that seem
precious, gleaming wet in the sun –

or showing friends where we sometimes hide
in the briar thicket, safe from prying
eyes, or on a high branch, death-defying

or down in the quarry, where the water falls
over trees and rocks and when Mummy calls
it sounds like a tiny voice inside

some other world, where grown-ups exist
and dream about all the fun they've missed.

*

2

Our Goldfinch

Our goldfinch in its cage
or flitting from lamp to chair,
spitting fury in its rage
or settling down in someone's hair

is still a pet, not wild
and therefore to be cherished
by both adult and child,
when it might have perished

in some gutter as a chick,
squashed by tyre of lorry,
too small to be quick,
too naïve to worry.

Therefore we sing its praises –
better safe than sorry.

*

I

Reading

As soon as I read my book
nothing else matters.
If someone says to me: Look
at this and that, he chatters
in vain. I say: Leave me be!
My reading is a reverie,

a dream halfway between
the world and my heart.
If someone says: Have you seen
my coat, my shoes, I say: Depart!
Make no further demand.
Let me read and understand.

*

2

Calvin and Hobbes

Once Calvin said to Hobbes: Look here,
it seems you don't know who I am.
I'm the king of Abyssinia
not a tiger or a lamb.
Bow down before my majesty
or I'll clobber you with my sword.
Said Hobbes: Let's do something else;
I'm bored.

Now Calvin was a patient lad
who liked to travel light.
He said: Come on, let's hit the road,
we'll not come back till night.
You'll be my lowly servant,
I'll be your mighty lord.
Said Hobbes: Let's do something else,
I'm bored.

* * *

What It Is

Oh the tiring, tiring lack of clarity!
The innumerable contests over next to nothing!
Why this icy wind that destroys all before it?
Is the world not a hard-boiled egg
Ready to be swallowed by the powerful egotist?
I would not be overstating my case by much
If I were to admit the following:
I am at my wits' end.
At one moment existence seems quite possible,
A little humour, a sense of fulfilment,
Even at times the knowledge that all is well,
And then that explosion in the living room,
A conflagration in the kitchen,
Clowns performing at my expense.
The pale sun of winter promising nothing.

I see snowy peaks at an immense distance,
Geese traversing the crystal sky.
I believe I can see myself now
Gently weaving down that powdery slope,
Brilliant sun, frost stinging the nostrils.
I prop my skis against the low branch of a pine,
Jab the poles through the crust,
Knock the snow off my jacket.

This is the true manna, enduring sustenance,
Preparation for the real light of day.
I open my eyes to the shimmering world,
Cornucopia of splendid opportunities for living.
The nameless beauty that clings to all I see.
What is death? A sieve. A filter.
And pain? Well, together we shall get through it.

*

A Toe Hold

'I can park in a small space
And I can back up a lovely trailer'.
God in his tender mercies
Allows me to boast of
One or two small accomplishments
As long as I leave the
Credit for the bigger ones to him.

*

A Stroll at Nightfall

At times it's enough to walk for the
Brain to come up with significant sequences.
The loadstar circles overhead
For those who reject the subliminal advantages.
Others prefer a frank discussion with the elements.

By a process of triangulation
I have achieved an emotional balance
Far surpassing that of the elephant-bearing turtle.

My maker and I take the next hill in stride here,
Up the Mountain Road, the wild-fowlers on the left,
A steady stream of traffic for a ground bass
And the twittering of a few late birds
Getting ready for nightfall.

There is a terrific dependence nowadays on
pre-cast world views.
Virulent intellectuals spice up their existence
With an ongoing analysis of historicity.
However the golden beech leaves underfoot
Rustle as heretofore
Or stick to the tarmac.

Moment after moment has its teeth
Pulled by official religions.
Granaries overflow,
Appetites are not satisfied,
However the sweet scent of smoke in the air
From distant bonfires in gardens
Where the leaves were raked
informs us of our productive mortality.

I alone seem to care about this,
Although that may be an illusion –
Fall-out from creative originality.

(I alone do not really exist,
So why make these pseudo-prophetic
announcements
To a world content in its cocoon!)

The orange light from street lamps
Gathers in diminishing puddles.
The salient features of the night
Impress themselves on the dead
and the living alike.
Nothing persuades like a pain in the lower back
Or the death of a friend.

It’s no longer possible to
Throw anything away nowadays
Without feeling conscience-bound
To buy something new. But look,
The storage cupboards are overflowing,
The shelves are creaking,
The larders are heavy with frozen goods,
The clothes rails groan under the
Weight of enough garments to
Clothe oneself six times over.

It’s dark now and I
Stumble over these grassy knolls –
My voice sounds strangely perfunctory.

Now thank heaven I’m back on the path,
The mythic path I know so well,
Just north of the quarry, between stiles,
From where I look down on the luminous town.

*

An Alarming Situation

(three poems)

1

Don't take it too seriously.
It is merely an avalanche,
A terror of the emotions,
Not to worry.

All the same I find it impossible
To march to this tune.
Reason goes out the window
And I feel put upon.

My nose is out of joint,
Children laugh at me.
I want to close my eyes
And disappear for a while.

How do these blazes get started!
On this topic I am
As ignorant as the next man
Who aims high.

Nature now is a mere speck,
A lone sail on the horizon
And as the sky darkens
I wish I were out there.

*

2

Can I bring my fear to book?
Would it annoy anyone
If I served up
The condition of being let down,
Utterly and completely,
By my wits?

It will not do to rage,
To bring charges against god
Or to pity oneself.
What exactly does that leave?
I ask, so that no one will ask me.

Suddenly the world turns upside down
And pain is the order of the day.
One wishes one could sway
Those who are responsible
Except that they do not exist.

I know I am never alone
And when I come to you
You arrange matters in such a way
That sooner or later
The world makes sense again.

Meanwhile I hold myself in readiness
For whatever is to come my way
On the back of these atrocious
Absurdities, these impossibilities
That demand to be confronted.

*

3

Action is not always possible.
Sometimes you just have to lie still
And wait for the axe to descend.
That is of course an image
Which should not be taken too seriously.

The locus vivendi, tragedy,
Impels us towards one another
And then in opposite directions.
I call that the work principle
And try to keep it in mind.

If words did not come my way,
Mitigating and comforting words,
I would surely despair.
The miracle of the rose is simply
The one that makes it grow.

* * *

Impressions at Lake Dhu

After a fortnight of drenching rain,
One of the first balmy evenings,
The sun at eight o'clock
Reflecting on the dark water
And a heron massively rising –
This boat left to drift
Among islands of irises;
In the distance blackbirds and larks.

The cows graze peacefully
As the first cooling breezes
Brush over the hillside.
A bluish mist shrouds meadows and hedges.

One swan is on the lake.

Gorse bush, ash tree and dry stone wall,
The gentle slope of a hill with hedge comb,
The sky turning lilac now and an orange sun
Casts its path of gold towards me
Across the water where the flies stay low now.
The far shore is black except for a nesting swan.

You can smell the farm from here,
The manure and the silage
Mingled with hawthorn and moist grass.

The traditional approach to this land
Is still the best by far,
Usage and stewardship,
Grateful earth residence
Reflecting merciful creation.

(When the shags have stooped to
Herding the trout like
Greedy fishermen in factory ships,
They must be eliminated.)

This lake is picturesque to the extreme,
Therefore readily symbolic,
Equally lending itself to
Sweet contemplation from the shore,
Where the midges dance
And I am too spellbound to recall
Ever being elsewhere –
Or to rowing leisurely
Within arm's length of the shore,
Water dripping from polished paddles
And the mind in a light of daydream.

Into an inlet
The boat slides smoothly.
Now shadows descend.
A tangle of willow branches
Snakes along black water.
Imagine a forest of irises and rushes, of
Mint, marestails and buttercup.
Hush, be as still as you can,
Let the truth speak,
Furnish your heart with memories.

Gorse bush, ash tree and dry stone wall,
The gentle slope of a hill with hedge comb,
The sky turning lilac and an orange sun
Casts its path of gold towards me
Across the water where the flies stay low now.
The far shore is black except for a nesting swan.

*

An immortal evening,
The lake slightly milky now,
A swallow sips from the surface –
The rush of invisible traffic –
A late tractor –

* * *

Time congealed *Nov. 2008*

The empty spaces between stars
seem empty to the naked eye,
all darkness interspersed with suns
and shivering ghosts,
and cursing demons at their posts.

But this is nonsense, I know,
not worthy to be put in words,
except on a night like the present,
where sleep is under attack
and my soul is on the rack.

No longer does existence
invite me to the dance.
I am a dull immobile thing,
spirit has flown the coop,
I am wilting, I droop.

My hope is for the morning,
for a little refreshment,
meanwhile I cannot rest.
Is it total exhaustion that plagues me
or life that begs me

to hold out for a moment longer
while changes are made to my flesh?
Suffer, says the spirit of life.
The reward will soon be revealed
when time has congealed.

*

All This Waiting *19/11/08*

If nothing else will do the trick,
Why not write yourself to sleep?
Waiting for the clock to tick
Builds up trials, but they'll keep.

Study the writing on the wall
Where the demon hand leaves traces.
Waiting for the sword to fall
Ruins your comfort, but it braces.

Over hill and dale you traipse,
Active inwardly exactly.
Waiting till the air escapes,
Conjures space and light, compactly.

All this waiting makes me wonder
Who is that approaching yonder?

*

You Speak *21/11/08*

You speak, your speech drifts heavenward
the while your thoughts remain on earth
and seven times your soul is worth
the grim gymnastics of the bard.

You speak and not a word remains
behind where populations drift.
Indeed you give the fool a lift,
the clown who gladly entertains.

You speak within a single frame
of god-refrain and world-renown.
The god who writes your language down
is not concerned but means the same

until judicious use of gold
advantage brings to young and old.

*

A late reflection 23/11/08

Very gradually I entrust myself
to this new ray of light.
A thousand apertures
let this light in.
If only my nerves hold out
you will not hear me complain.
I dream of distant places
where mountains are reflected
in the still, blue waters of a lake.

*

Oh do not speak of growing old   24/11/08

As certain as the stars that shine
Is your love and I depend on it.
What we two have been up to
Over the many years of our friendship
Is not worth discussing
Because it does not amount to the
Sort of history people refer to as
Glorification of the past.
Instead let us be grateful
That the snows have not covered our traces
And that the kingdom is now known to us.

Perpetual music stimulates our hearts
And far into the night do we recall
Our exploration of the wild country
Where chastity was comparatively unknown
And dreaming assassins ran amok
On snowfields and on the fragrant prairie.

Now that the moon over the fishing villages
Brings lovers out onto the perfumed sea
In their elaborately carved dugouts
Wreathed in acanthus leaves as in
Ancient Corinth or on the blood-drenched
Fields of sun-burnt Thessalonica
And the men trim their beards after
A day in the grape trenches
Making ready for a night of carousing,
We discover again in each other's eyes
The revealed splendour of our affection.

Oh do not speak of growing old and dying
For each day is still, as always,
A fresh acquaintance with our god
And a greater appreciation of our partnership.

*

A little rest, my Lord *30/11/08*

Settle down, soul,
you cause me too much pain.
I am the tree
sensing the next quake in my roots.
Clouds rain down on me,
mists engulf me.
I am the lighthouse,
the breakers foam up on me,
the moon hastens over the horizon.

If only I had no more wishes!
Why can I not just
tell my heart to stop beating!
The strength is gone from me,
the cheer and merriment.
Sorrow and anguish
struggle for space in me
though I see no reason.

A little rest, my Lord,
to see me out of the day!
Warmth of emotion, please,
to send me to sleep.
Is there no end to this struggle
for the superlative life,
agony, heroic decisions
in dead earnest and a broad smile
on the enemies pusillanimous face ?

*

The Voyage Continues *02/12/08*

When all is well,
the mind is working smoothly and
the body knows no fear,
we are bound to wonder
how can we tie this down?
This state must be prolonged,
so which button do I push?
The laughter of several angels
rings in the marble hall;
we are invited to laugh at ourselves.

No, the voyage continues
through thick and thin,
over the bodies of the
slaughtered enemy, then
down that dark passageway
called senescence by some,
except that it leads
out into that perfect land
where even tragedy is amusing.

It needs to be made clear
that darkness is a stage,
that pain is a sign,
that unhappiness is an introduction.
Oh I know, we struggle
and sleep in the bed we made
but every performance gains us
a title to some unknown acreage
held for us in trust
by the one whose love is creative.

*

Suddenly terror rose

Suddenly terror rose out of the
furry surface of a dark
emotion and we sank to our knees
like executed prisoners of war.

The red foam drew our attention
as it spread over mood after mood,
clinging with raptorial tenacity
to our icy fingers as we reached for it.

The booming voice out of the sky
was too loud to be perceived; it only
paralyzed what was left of our souls
and then god's hand brushed us aside.

*

Sink down

Sink down into your idle individuality
where the wild dogs pace back and forth
outside the perimeter fence
silently, certain of their quarry.

Once again the moon rises
golden in my brain, where Orion
dips behind every sweet memory,
forcing my delusions to the fore.

Indeed with our heightened awareness
we may pump the earth full of significance
so that even the midge and the inchworm
may participate in the certainty of our dreams.

*

I sink back

26/12/08

Along the lamp-lit alleyway
While in the houses children sing
I make my way reluctantly
Conscious of this one single thing:

However I behave and dream
There's language to console my heart
And while I cannot dance for you
Or show you outwardly I care

I speak to every natural thing
That grows in my vicinity
For me and for all who like myself
Disport themselves human-naturally.

The north wind scatters yellowing leaves
From oak and birch because their time
Has come like also mine must come
When I no longer think in speech

But being enlightened by your face
I sink back from my human will;
I hasten to your sweet embrace
And all is filled and all is done.

*

Finding myself at the centre *03/01/09*

Finding myself at the centre
I imbibe my environment.
The structured world stands to one side,
Smoking in the twilight.
Monstrous clouds swallow jets,
Messages bombard my carapace,
A crocodile eyes me suspiciously.

If I tell you of my predicament
Will you hug it to your breast
And sweetly whisper into its ear
What you have always wished from your
Best friend while you drowned in shame?
Can you imagine what I mean?

Finding myself at the centre
I make reparation for past neglect.
Some say that our flesh absorbs
Our god's tender mercies willingly,
However we travel to distant lands
To make one enemy, when here and now
The likeliest of them lurks in our heart.

*

On a Mild Sunday Morning

On a mild November Sunday morning,
only one man on the street in front of me,
and the seagulls playful in the clouds,
I draw fresh air into my lungs
and stretch my legs in imitation of youthfulness.

I kick at a few stones,
a splinter of glass that tinkles along the paving
and see myself vivid as a boy on the football pitch,
when nothing mattered except exuberant
companionship
and plenty of sport to give the lie to survival.

Off South Street the canal makes its way
towards Strangford Lough, today
no more than a trickle of clear water
over an assortment of rubbish:
wheel rims, beer tins, a discarded umbrella –
a robin dives headlong over the railing.

The leaves of a couple of stunted oaks
                                        on the opposite bank
are beginning to crinkle and yellow.
A spent buddleia, with dismal brown flower heads,
prepares for winter in a corner where two walls meet.

This is the mood beyond question
and around here I feel hopelessly at ease.
My eye lights on a spring gushing out of a mud bank,
to me a fascinating symbol of new life,
while the tolling of the bell from the tower of
Strean Church sanctions the old.

I exchange a few words with a couple of drunks
nursing their bottles in comfort in the ditch.
They tell me Christmas is coming.

A young man with a face like ten days of rain
is evidently taking his young son for a walk.
Over to the east, on the flats,
the airport seems busy this morning.

I find myself on a grassy path
behind a defunct factory. Now look at this!
Someone has taped a bouquet of carnations
to that steel fence. I wonder who died here –
I march on; no time for sentiment this morning.

Two pairs of little girls' shoes and a schoolbag
lie discarded among the thistles and high grass.
I bet there's a story in that.

Nothing much moves me this morning;
we all have days like this.
I notice wild radish blooming on a heap of brown soil
and shepherd's purse too. This time of year?

Fresh green ivy
Snakes up a corrugated brown painted fence
Across recent graffiti.

A car-boot sale adjacent to the football ground
seems to be in full swing.
I confess I am idly curious.
I stray past the stands,
past displays of bric-a-brac,
of second hand boots and army medals,
of shabby glitz for yet another Christmas.

I love to see all this junk,
this fag-end of a folk memory.
No one seems to care whether they sell anything;
the idea is to live in expectation.

Now through Londonderry park,
Scrabo hill and tower in the distance.
Clear sky overhead,
clouds bearing down over the Lough.

I'm not so silly as to assume
that this will interest anyone but myself,
however sometimes we have to give voice
to a few preliminary statements,
otherwise the soul collapses
as it loses its familiarity with the creative process.

I cross the canal again and the stench
once more takes me back to my childhood,
when I vacuumed impressions in,
not discriminating between wealth and rot.

The finery of many an obligation since then
has weighed me down and brought me to my senses.
I wonder do you know what I mean.
A redshank perches on the top rail of a fence
on the opposite side of the canal.
It dips and bobs and says: "Oh yes…oh yes."

* * *

Silent Shadows *02/07/10*

Only what I know
Has helped me prosper.
Now, here where I live
I turn my face
Skyward, homeward.

Oh I have my fill
Of vast experience,
Life, death in my hand
And pain that bears
Much fruition.

Silent shadows creep
Inside me heart-ward,
Each full in itself
Of terror, shame,
Blood and mercy.

*

Oh child of mine … *12/28/'04*

Why don't you do as you're told,
You little child of mine?
I speak, you hear –
Then you disappear,
As if you cared not one whit.
I wonder what is the cause of it.

The child leans on its little feet
And looks for all the world as if
It thought and thought:
Such happiness as you have brought
Into my life I count
Precious but there's not much.

I am still mulling over
My time in the womb
Where I never had to ask
For food or drink.
I think and think
But nothing much comes of it.

Who knows what it takes
To lead a child astray
Or in the proper way?
The abnormalities cost
More than we're willing to confess,
And so too the wantonness.

*

One last time *13/01/'05*

Evening,
Singing the day's concerns,
The burning questions,
One last time.

Oh immortal ones
Give me to drink,
I by myself cannot
Solve these problems.

The benign one looks down
From within as always,
Points out the route
For the stressed soul.

Then I assert myself
One last time
In perfect faith,
Renewing wholeness.

*

No Echo 13/01/'05

No echo,
Shouting into distance
Produces no echo,
Only encouragement.

Slowly the gate opens,
The brief encounter
Recorded since youth
Has benefited.

Still no echo,
This to assure us,
To reject the fainthearted
For approach another time.

Slowly the gate closes,
Now we are safe;
Distances and nearness
Are one.

*

Outstayed your welcome *12/02/'11*

But I long for a change.
As the broad street narrows
and the violations refuse to be forgotten,
I cannot make sense of the way these
monotonous recurrences confront me:

The shameful pattern of deceit
makes of each day one long hallucination.
I step carefully or run,
the prize eludes me all the same,
the game mocks me through

walls of fog, screams
abuse down from the heights of
rocky outcrops, looks open-eyed
when I suddenly round a corner,
then ducks out of sight.

My life has lost its taste.
If I knew where my real interests lay
I could exert myself that way
but though I return with each breath
to the centre of the atmosphere

the bitter resentment holds sway:
You do not belong here.
You have outstayed your welcome.
The very way you sit and hang your hand
is considered an outrage.

* * * * *

Index of titles in alphabetic order **page**

* * *

www.ingramcontent.com/pod-product-compliance
Ingram Content Group UK Ltd.
Pitfield, Milton Keynes, MK11 3LW, UK
UKHW020230250726
13967UKWH00001B/283